# Get ready! You need:

1. A ~~small~~ very big heart ♥

   BOOM BOOM
   BOOM BOOM
   BOOM BOOM

2. A full pencil case

   Pencils mandatory!

3. A taste for adventure

   Hop aboard the tour bus! We're on our way — with twists and turns — to the land of love and friendship.

   VROOM! VROOM!

# Decipher the coooooool 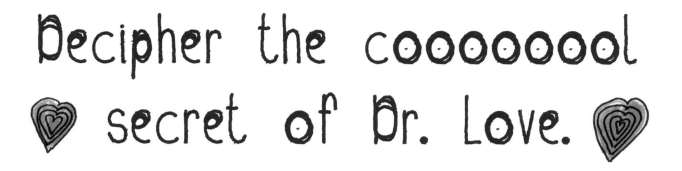 secret of Dr. Love.

It's easy! Just add some "o"s (like "Oooooooooohhhhhh, I really love your shoes!").

THE M_RE Y_U L_VE PE_PLE, THE M_RE BEAUTIFUL Y_UR LIFE WILL BE!

The famous Dr. Love, world's greatest authority on love and friendship. (University of Kisstown, CA)

Answer:
The more you love people, the more beautiful your life will be!

# WHO ARE PEOPLE?

Cross out all the people, except for yourself,
and see what's left...

(like this)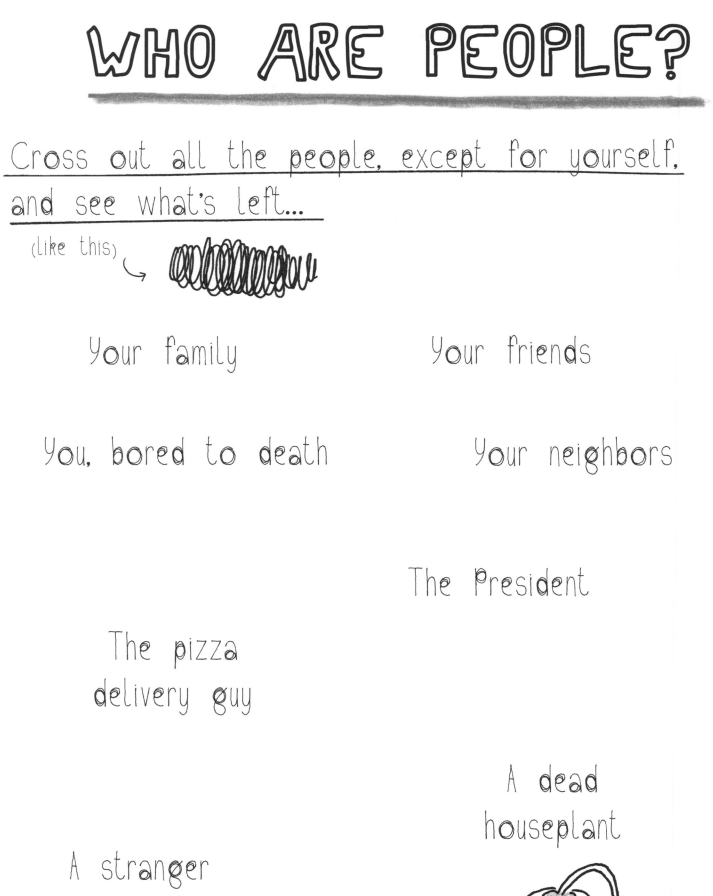

Your family

Your friends

You, bored to death

Your neighbors

The President

The pizza
delivery guy

A dead
houseplant

A stranger
crossing the
street

# WHO ARE NOT?

Your favorite
comic book heroes

Your boyfriend/
girlfriend

A huge,
dead rat →

The Chinese

The French

# SNIFF!!

Answer:

The only things left are: you, bored to death, a dead houseplant, and a huge, dead rat. How sad!

# Are you always ready

1

Imagine you were taking a walk and you ran into an alien...

Hello! BZIZIZI BZIZIZIZIZI Can you show me around?

# to meet new people?

Even weirdos?

2

What would you do?

☐ You act nonchalant and say, "No problem, Mr. Alien. Let's go!"

☐ You run away, screaming, "Mommy!!! Mommy!!! A hideous alien!"

☐ You don't even have the time to run away because you've already disappeared.

If you checked this box, great! You're very open-minded and will always be able to make new friends.

# What goes together?

Connect the things that belong together.
(You can use the same people to connect with
more than one thing.)

example :

The baker *

Your family *

Your friends *

Santa Claus *

Your teacher *

The dentist *

Your favorite celebrities *

* Delicious confections

* Knowledge

* Love

* Encouragement

* Presents

* Education

* Security

* A joke

* Dreams

* Kindness

* Arguments

* Occasional punishment

* Help and comfort

* A house and clothes

* Friendship

* Occasional pain

* Compliments

Don't worry if your page is a tangled mess! It just means that you know lots of people who bring lots of things to your life!

What about you? What **do you do** for other people?

Make a list.

examples :
This week, I'm going to share my snack with . . . . . . . . . . .
I made a joke . . . . . . . . . .
I punched . . . . . . . . . . .

- 
- 
- 
- 
- 

You see! All these people would be really sad if you weren't around!

# World's Greatest Quiz!

## How many people live on planet Earth ?

Don't forget to count your worst enemy!

- [ ] 2
- [ ] 3,258
- [ ] 15,233
- [ ] 7,821,966
- [ ] over 5 million
- [ ] around 7 billion
- [ ] 250 million billion

Answer :

Around 7 billion. Whoa! That's a lot!

# An Important Question

## What's the difference between:

① Loving something that's alive

Your grandmother

Your dog

② Loving an object

Answer:

Living things love you back, but objects don't, so don't get too attached to those!

Could you give me a hug?

# A Seriously Philosophical Page

| Love is when... | Friendship is when... |
| --- | --- |
|  |  |

Write down everything you can think of!

# Does everyone bug you sometimes?

(Even the people that you usually adore?)

YES ☐ Don't worry, it's normal.
It happens to everyone.
Quick, look at the next page!

→

NO ☐ What a liar!
Or ... What's your secret?

# Here are some ideas to help you relax!

You can also show your parents this page when they're stressed out!

Close your eyes and breathe deeply through your nose 10 times.

Read a book.

Take a hot bath and belt out your favorite song.

Relax, baby!

Say this to yourself 50 times.

Get some exercise.

Drink a really strong cup of coffee.

## Circle the really bad idea!

# Make an address book.

**1** Buy a notebook.

**2** Paste a piece of blank paper on the cover and decorate it.

My Best Friends

Write down all of your friends' phone numbers and addresses, or I'll eat you!

Really handy for:

homework          invitations

# ✳ Another Riddle ✳

Find the two things a best friend and
a priceless porcelain vase have in common:

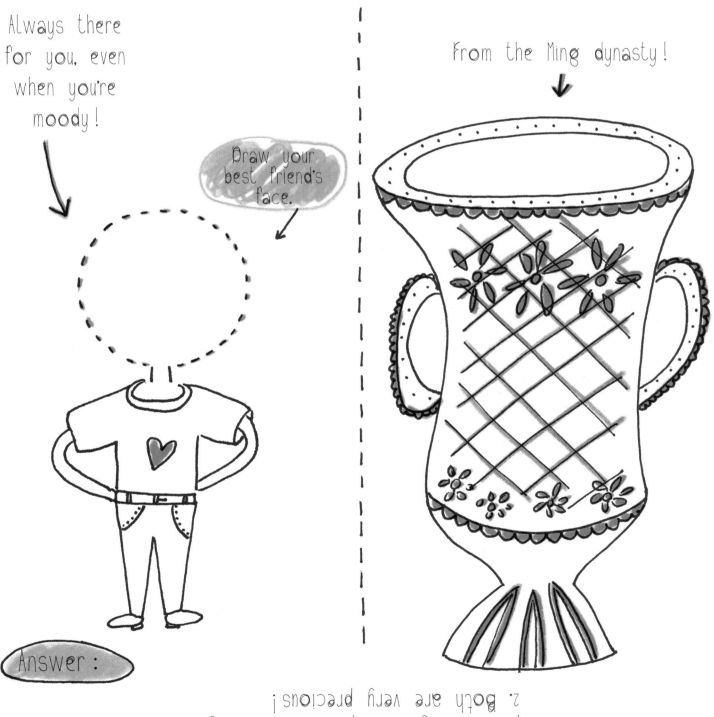

Always there
for you, even
when you're
moody!

From the Ming dynasty!

Draw your
best friend's
face.

Answer:

1. Both are very fragile and can break into a thousand
pieces if you drop them suddenly.
2. Both are very precious!

# Who would you like to be friends with?

## Justin

- Sharp dresser
- Great hair
- Always in style
  (even when he's just making toast)
- Thinks only about himself!
- Talks only about himself!
- Great at rollerblading

## Kate

- Extremely smart
- Doesn't seem very funny
- A little shy
- Really nice when you get to know her

## Noah

- Knows nothing about style
- Owns 2 T-shirts and 2 pairs of pants
- Very generous
- Very funny

## Brittany

- Really pretty
- Often mistaken for Miss America
- Never smiles
- Wants the entire school to fall at her feet
- Creates problems when there aren't any

## Drew

- Knows a bunch of incredible stories
- Always ready for adventure
- Horrible at math
- Spends her vacations at camp
- Really super nice

## Sophia

- Great smile
- Too cute
- Always enthusiastic (especially about pranks)
- Super loyal friend
- Doesn't have a TV at her house

Don't be fooled by appearances!
Choose your friends for what
they're like, not how they look!

# Describe how you met your best friend.

their

name →

# ? Why do you like ? them so much?

# Create a friendship pact with your BFF.

Directions:

1. Cut out the next page.
2. Fill it out.
3. Make a copy.
4. You and your BFF sign both copies.
5. You and your BFF each keep a copy.

# SUPER FRIENDSHIP PACT

We, the undersigned: ✓ your names ↘

_____ and _____

declare we are the best friends in the world.
Here is a list of things we do together to prove it.
(example: We never tell people our most intimate secrets.)

① 

② 

③ 

④ 

⑤ 

Made in duplicate: _____ ← place

on: _____ ← date

Each BFF writes, reads, approves and signs in a box.

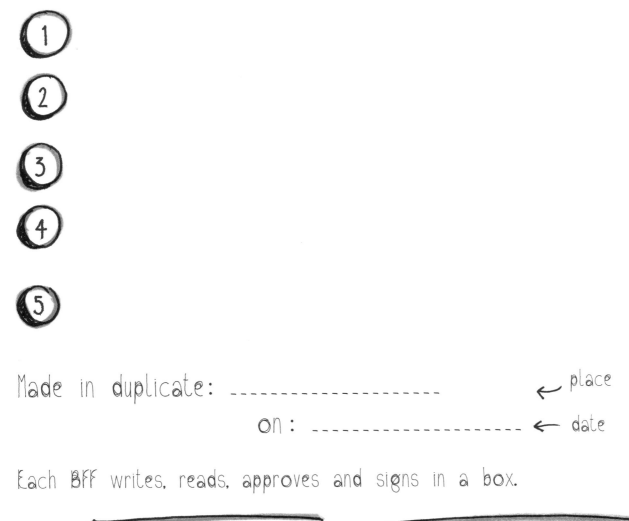

(This is the back of
the Super Friendship Pact.)

# Record-Breaking Laughs

List your top 3 best laughs:

| Sound | Who I was with | Duration |
|-------|----------------|----------|
| ① | | |
| ② | | |
| ③ | | |

haha!

hehe!

hoho!

 **2** You've got 30 seconds to figure out who your best friends are. Next, draw the 10 friends you've decided to save and a captain for the lifeboat.

Draw yourself with a cap.

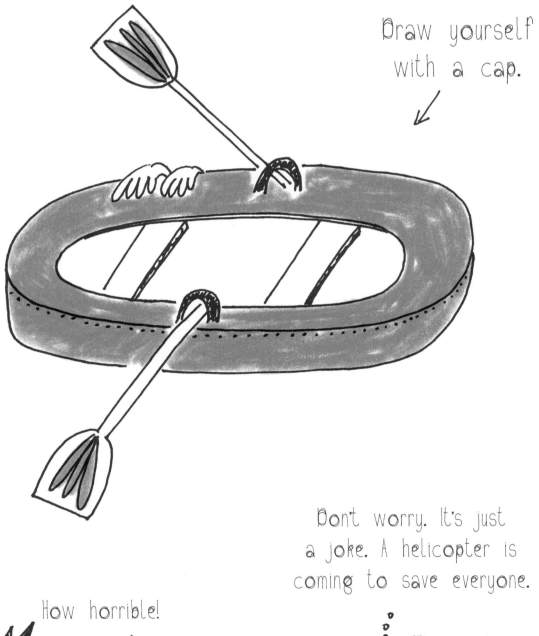

Don't worry. It's just a joke. A helicopter is coming to save everyone.

How horrible!

# Create a cool club for yourself and all of your friends!

Club's name →

Members ↘

Club's mission ↘

Club's motto ↓

Club's logo ↘

What club members like to do
(nothing too mean or nasty!)

Club's theme song (idea: Take a song you know and change the lyrics.)

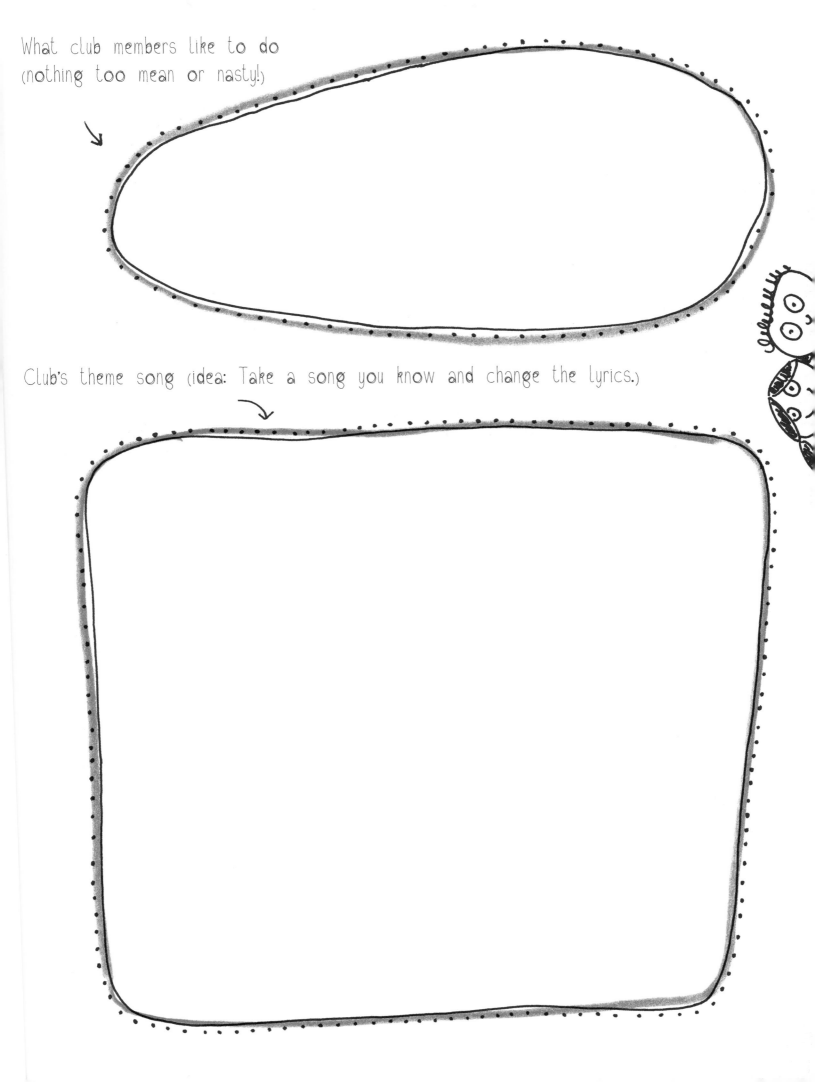

# Photo Friend-zy!

1 Take pictures of your friends and stick them in the boxes below.

2 Change them with a black marker.
Scribble wigs, mustaches, glasses and vampire teeth!

Write their names on the dotted lines. →

click! click! Don't forget a picture → of yourself!

MAKE UP A SONG TO LIFT YOUR SPIRITS!

If you want to be friends with someone, but they don't, make up a little song and sing it to yourself whenever you feel down.

their name

I don't care about you — — — — —
it's true.

— — — — — were're not friends and
I'm not blue.

— — — — — too bad you don't know
what you're missing.

I'm going to try to forget
all about you — — — — —

Life is cool for me, without
you — Phew!

# A list of my best pranks!

Describe the funniest pranks
you've ever played:

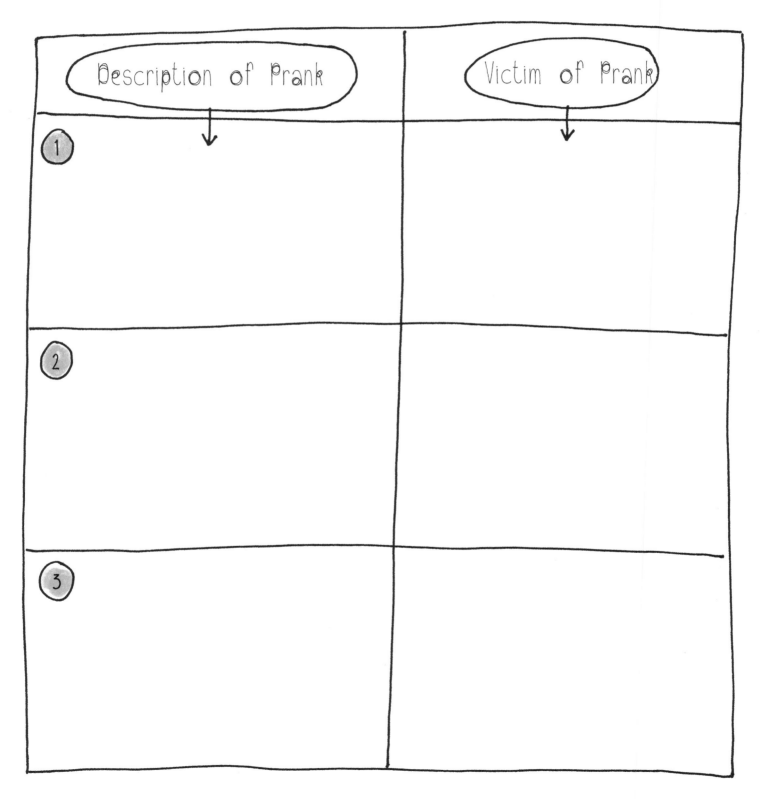

| Description of Prank | Victim of Prank |
|---|---|
| 1 | |
| 2 | |
| 3 | |

# A list of the best times I've had with my friends!

## Describe your favorite activities:

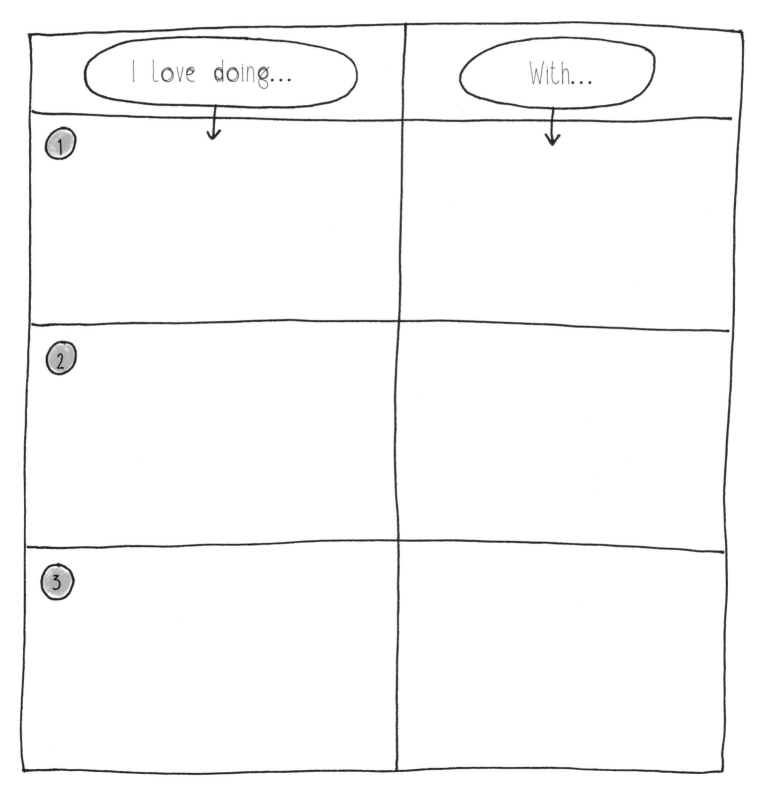

| I love doing... | With... |
|---|---|
| 1 | |
| 2 | |
| 3 | |

**HOW HORRIBLE!**

**1** Someone showed up at school wearing the latest amazing pair of tennis shoes. The exact same tennis shoes you've been dreaming about for the past three days.

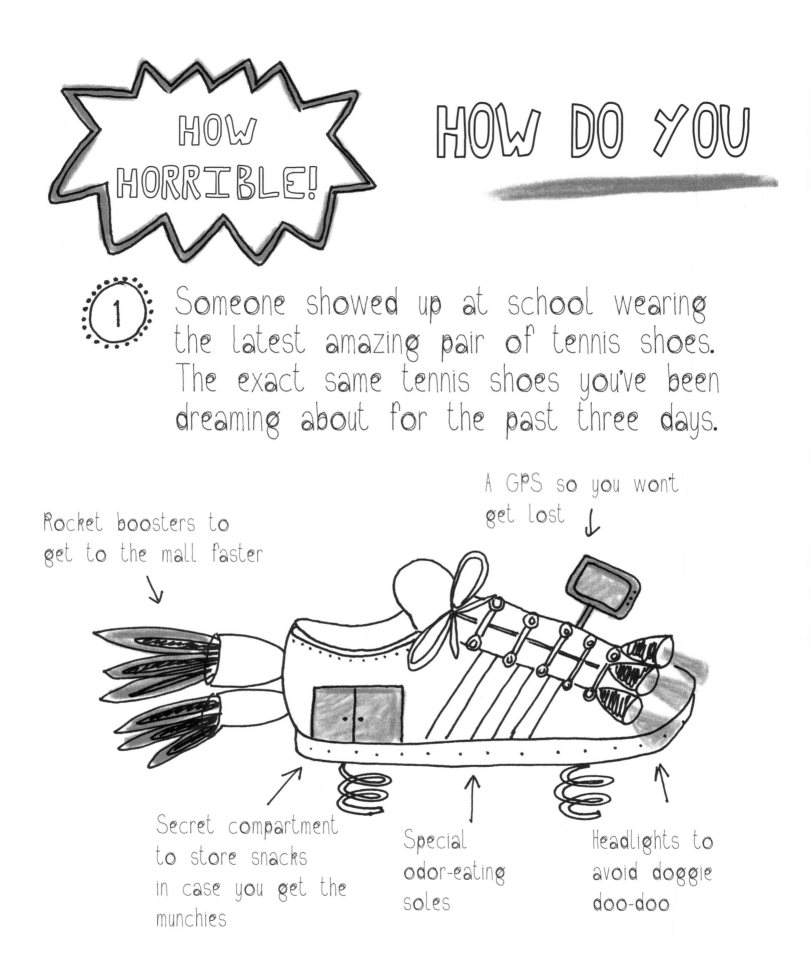

A GPS so you won't get lost ↓

Rocket boosters to get to the mall faster ↓

Secret compartment to store snacks in case you get the munchies

Special odor-eating soles

Headlights to avoid doggie doo-doo

# DEAL WITH JEALOUSY?

**②** Select the response that won't make you look like a spoiled brat:

**a** Green with envy, you have a meltdown in class. At home that night, you do the same in front of your parents and scream that you want the same shoes right now!

**b** You say nothing, but you think to yourself that life is unfair, really, really unfair. You'd rather die from a broken heart in the middle of the cafeteria (right after dessert).

**c** You tell yourself that after all, they're just a pair of shoes, and in two days they won't be in style anyway.

The best reaction:

c

# Here's a very, very, very personal question: Do you feel really lonely sometimes

If you do, describe the situation:
(example: when you tell a funny joke and nobody laughs)

Don't worry about it!
It happens to everyone!

A horrible, old sock

# Have your friends over for a cozy slumber party.

Cross out the 2 (or 3) things that are not completely necessary for a great sleepover.

An extra mattress

A really comfy pillow

love

A comforter or sleeping bag

A bottle of expensive champagne and a pound of caviar

A little nightlight in case someone is afraid of the dark

An extra set of pajamas and a toothbrush

A bearskin rug that your dad brought home from Siberia

Your Sleepover
Survival Kit
(everything you need to
bring to a slumber party)

1. Cross out the things you don't need, then fill in the box.

2. Cut out the page and hang it in your room.

# My Sleepover Survival Kit

(a) My favorite pajamas or nightgown

(b) My favorite underwear

(c) All my pets

(d) My toothbrush and toothpaste

(e) A fabulous change of clothes

(f) Somes chips and cookies in case the dinner is gross

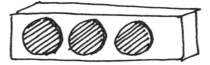

(g) My mom

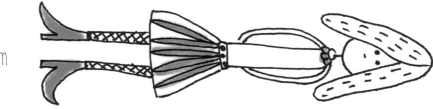

and ... →

(This is the back
of the Sleepover Survival Kit.)

(This is the back
of the Sleepover Survival Kit.)

# Proper Etiquette

**Cross out the things you shouldn't say when you visit a friend's house.**

* Hello, everyone. Thanks for the invite.

* It's really ugly here. Did your mom decorate?

* What's that green thing on my dish?

* No, thank you. It's really good, but I'm not hungry.

* Nah! I'm not going to help clear the dishes. I'm not your slave!

* Oh, I slept horribly. Must have been the bed.

* I really had a great time. Thanks a lot.

Arrghh !!!
That kid has no manners. I don't want him to set foot in this house ever again, understand?

# Test: Are you always prepared to help others?

• • • • • • • • • • • • •

Someone in your gym class has slipped on a banana peel. Both their arms, plus their head and their ears are in a cast. You :

|  | | Yes | No |
|---|---|---|---|
| a | help them carry their backpack. | ☐ | ☐ |
| b | help them eat their lunch. | ☐ | ☐ |
| c | take advantage of the situation and steal their dessert. | ☐ | ☐ |
| d | write nice things on their cast. | ☐ | ☐ |
| e | do their homework for them. | ☐ | ☐ |
| f | take advantage of the fact they can't run very fast and draw mustaches and hair all over them. | ☐ | ☐ |

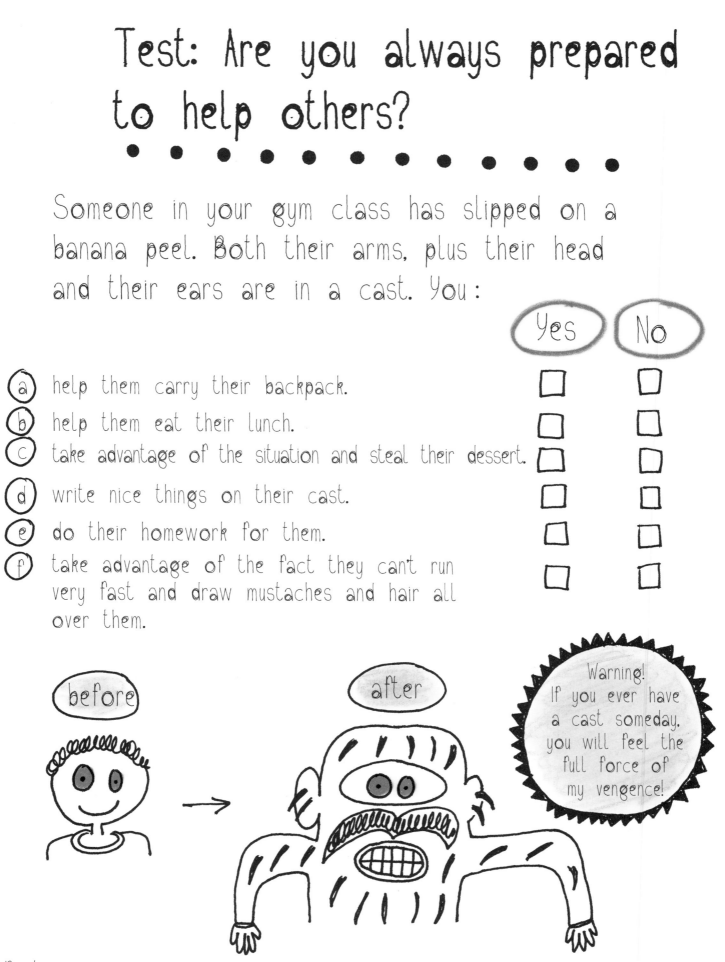

before

after

Warning! If you ever have a cast someday, you will feel the full force of my vengence!

Best responses:

a=Yes  b=Yes  c=No  d=Yes  e=Yes  f=No

# School Emergency!
## (Banana Peel Test)

You catch your best friend having a great time with your worst enemy. After snacking on a banana, what should you do with the peel?
(Check one of the boxes)

errrrrrr rrrrrrrr

a ☐ You drop the banana peel right under the foot of your worst enemy.
Result: 3 broken teeth and blood everywhere
+ your best friend won't talk to you anymore
+ you are suspended from school for 3 days

b ☐ You hold back your feelings, say nothing, but suffer inside.

c ☐ You ignore them. Later, you ask your best friend what was going on.

the banana peel, used as police evidence →

The best response:
c. Because it's always better to remain calm and talk things over!

# Make Your Own Party Invitations!

**Materials:**
- White or colored construction paper
- Glitter
- Fluorescent or silver markers

→ Cut the construction paper in half, fold it over and decorate it.

You're Invited!
date --*-- time
Get ready to party!

Clearly state the date and time.

An example for the inside

Your name here

Cool graphics

Bring your dancing shoes and your appetite!

Address

RSVP
to
before

Your address

Phone #

Date

Handmade invitations are cooler and much more personal than ones you print from your computer!

If your parents never want you to invite your friends over, or they don't let you go to your friends' houses, write your name on the dotted line and give them this note:

It is imperative that
_ _ _ _ _ invites his friends over and visits his friends at their homes a lot. A lack of fun can stunt a child's growth and can even cause them to shrink. See evidence below:

3 inches

Lily Lilliput,
43 years old.
Never had the right to see her friends when she was a kid.

Signed: Dr. Love

(This is the back
of the note to your parents.)

# It's Fun to Share!

## Invite three friends to share these delicious cakes.

The cake of your dreams, smothered in whipped cream!

Mini version

Strawberry tart

Strawberry tart that's been licked by a dog

## How should you start?

Watch out! You might get sick.

(cicle the right answer)

a) You make the first selection.

b) You let your friends pick first, and you take the last cake.

c) You turn off the lights and say, "Dig in!"

The correct answer :

b) But you could also cut each cake into 4 pieces. That way it's fair, and everyone's happy.

# Invite Your Friends Over for a Snack!

HOW NICE!

## 1 Set the table.

Put a large piece of white paper on the table so everyone can doodle on it!

Hide jokes and riddles in the napkins. →

HAHAHAHA HOHOHO

← Tape funny labels onto the glasses.

Whoever drinks from this glass is cool.

Change the soda bottle labels. →

Friendship Club Soda: The more you drink, the friendlier you'll be!

2

# Prepare a peanut butter pizza covered with M&M's® and colored sprinkles.

You need: 1 package of pizza dough and 1 jar of peanut butter
+ 1 large bag of plain M&M's®
+ 1 bottle of sprinkles

1. Prepare the pizza dough → by following the directions on the package.

2. Preheat the oven (make sure you get an adult to help). Cook the pizza crust according to the directions. →

3. Remove the pizza crust when it's cooked and let it cool.

→ 4. Spread a nice, thick layer of peanut butter on top and decorate it with the M&M's® and colored sprinkles.

Color the pizza!

# Name Game

Make a list of your friends' names,
then write them backwards!

| The Right Way | Switch it Up! |
|---|---|
| ex.: John Smith | Nhoj Htims |

Too funny!
They look like Martian names!

# BRAIN SHOCKER!

## Can you define these words?

Forgiving:

Even-tempered:

Solidarity:

Compassion:

Sociable:

Comfort:

You can use a dictionary or ask an adult
for help. Don't worry if you don't know, but
you'll need to learn them before the next game.

← Use the previous page for help.

# MATCH THE WORDS

① You are <u>forgiving</u> if...

② You are <u>even-tempered</u> if...

③ Showing <u>solidarity</u> is...

④ Showing <u>compassion</u> is...

⑤ You are <u>sociable</u> if..

⑥ You are <u>comforting</u> when...

example

# WITH THE CORRECT SITUATIONS

(a) You're always in a good mood.
(Even when you get a bad grade.)

→ (b) You're not mad if a friend borrows your new sweatshirt and returns it with holes in it.

(c) You love to invite lots of friends over for parties!

(d) When your friend has a meltdown, you have one too so they don't feel alone.

(e) When your friend Priscilla's hamster passes away, you feel her pain.

(f) You take Priscilla in your arms, give her a hug and say, "I'm sure you miss him very much."

Answers:
1-b, 2-a, 3-d, 4-e, 5-c, 6-f

# ✱ Can you keep a secret? ✱

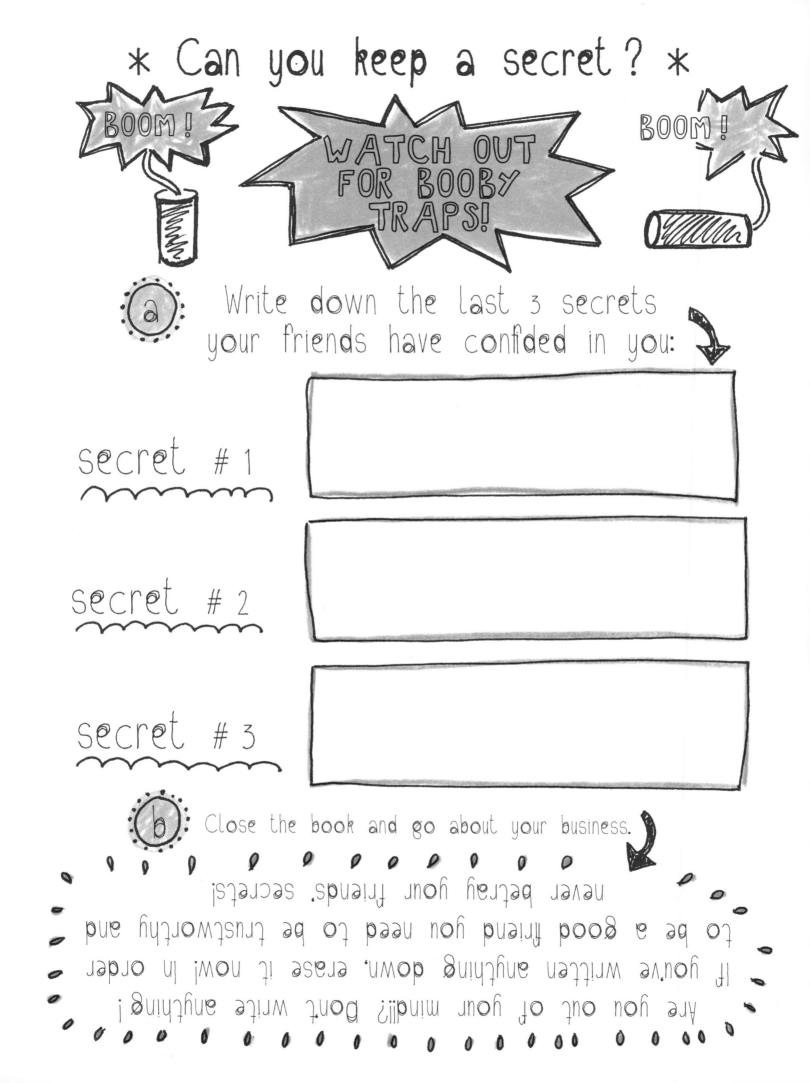

BOOM!

WATCH OUT FOR BOOBY TRAPS!

BOOM!

(a) Write down the last 3 secrets your friends have confided in you:

secret #1

secret #2

secret #3

(b) Close the book and go about your business.

Are you out of your mind?! Don't write anything! If you've written anything down, erase it now! In order to be a good friend you need to be trustworthy and never betray your friends' secrets!

# A brilliantly nasty idea:

Write something horrible on one of your classmates' back.

Stop it right now!
That's really mean and silly!
(Unless of course it's April 1st, which would make it funny!)

(Sometimes this book's author has stupid ideas.)

# Test of the Century

## Do you like it when:

| | | Yes | No |
|---|---|---|---|
| a | People make fun of you? (Or your braces?) | ☐ | ☐ |
| b | People give you really nice compliments? (example: "Whoa! Nice hair!") | ☐ | ☐ |
| c | People pick on your friend or boyfriend/girlfriend? | ☐ | ☐ |
| d | You're the only person that's not invited to an amazing New Year's Eve party? | ☐ | ☐ |

If you haven't checked off the correct boxes you are really strange and need some help! ☺

Answers:

a-No  b-yes  c-No  d-No

# A little game
# about your worst enemy

ⓐ

Draw them here.

# Find at least 3 good qualities about this person.

Mandatory! (If it's too difficult, take a break and try again later. You have to finish!)

1 ⟶ . . . . . . . . . . . . . . .

2 ⟶ . . . . . . . . . . . . . .

3 ⟶ . . . . . . . . . . . . . .

# A Universal Declaration

Memorize this by heart!
Bring this book to class
and share it with
the other kids.

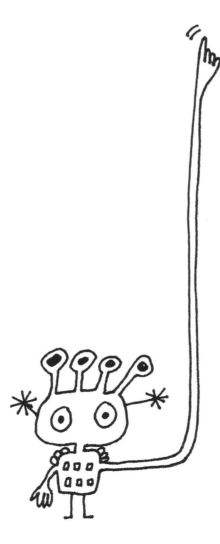

# of People's Rights

All human beings
Born all over the world
Dwarves and giants
Of all Nations
Everyone is the same.
In wheelchairs
On flying carpets
Oh yeah, all over the planet
All the people.
The ugly and the beautiful
The funny and not so funny
But who cares?
Because under the skin
We're all beautiful.
It doesn't matter what's outside
Because it's what's inside that counts
(la la la la la).
We all have the same heart
We all want to be happy.

# Dr. Love's Incredible Prescription

Professor Raymond Love
University of Kissland
Big Heart, California
contact: kisskisssmack@loveyourself.com

**1** Think hard and make a list of the things you really love about yourself. If you have trouble coming up with things, ask your parents for help.

**2** Think about this list a lot.

**3** When you look at yourself in the mirror while you're brushing your teeth, say this:

Whoa! I am too cool!

**4** This prescription must be refilled until you really, truly love yourself!

Dr. Love's signature ➡

# Are you Shy?

Make a list of the people you'd like to talk to, but haven't.

example: saying "Hi" to the most popular kid in school

(You can think about this without writing anything down if you're afraid someone will read it.)

# The Cure

**1**

Take a good look at this bottle. Now imagine drinking a spoonful of this potion every morning while repeating :
"I'm not afraid of anything !"

Magic
Anti-shyness
Potion
(fruit flavor)

**2**

This machine gives you a kick in the backside.

on
off

Put your cute little tush here.

**Go on!**

**You can do it!**

# The Killer Question!
## Bang! Bang!

Do you ever say or do things that you don't mean, just to make other people happy?

Example: You dress like a rock star even though you're really conservative.

Never ☐          A lot ☐

Always ☐    Sometimes ☐

➡ If you responded sometimes, a lot, or always, write down some examples!

# Revelation of the day:

You don't have to please everyone!
It's impossible!
Just be yourself!

# Don't Be Intimidated
# by Other People!

## Draw the biggest bully or showoff in your school.

Give them huge ears that stick out and lots of hair on their nose.

So, do you still feel the same about them?

# Make a list of the people you admire most.

Who | Why

You can write the names of all your heroes, even if they are not real people.

# The Horrible Story of

(Rated for ages 9+)

Once upon a time, there was a herd of sheep walking off a cliff.

When the first sheep (who was admired by the rest) fell off the cliff, the others heard her cry out.

They thought this was incredibly funny and rushed to follow her without giving it a second thought.

# What kind of people like to argue with you?

- 
- 
- 
- 
-

# What do you argue about most?

- 
- 
- 
- 

Ben, the
famous rat

↓

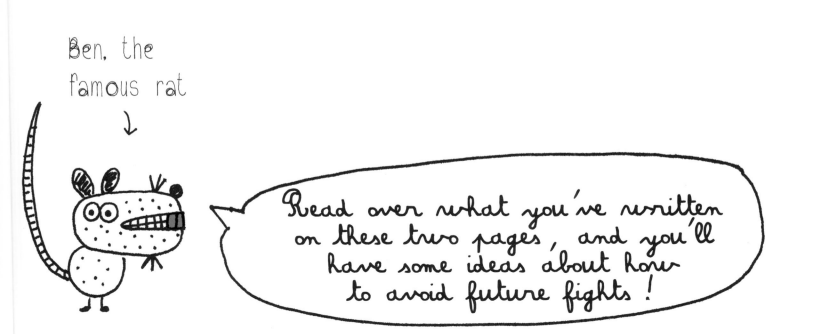

Read over what you've written on these two pages, and you'll have some ideas about how to avoid future fights!

# Making Up

Imagine that you've had a fight with your best friend.

## Option A
You invite him to your birthday party anyway.

At first, you're stressed.

But everyone is having fun !!!

He invites you to his birthday party next Saturday.

Everything is great. You have an amazing time together.

## Option B
You don't invite him to your birthday party.

He's really sad.

With a heavy heart, he worries all day long.

You are not invited to his birthday party. Sweet revenge!

Next Saturday, everyone is having fun except you. It's horrible!

And the moral of this tale is...

# ¡s Fun to Do!

Do you think it's possible to make up with someone after you've been mad at them for:

check one box

Yes    No

5 minutes
2 hours
3 days
3 months
1 year
all of your life

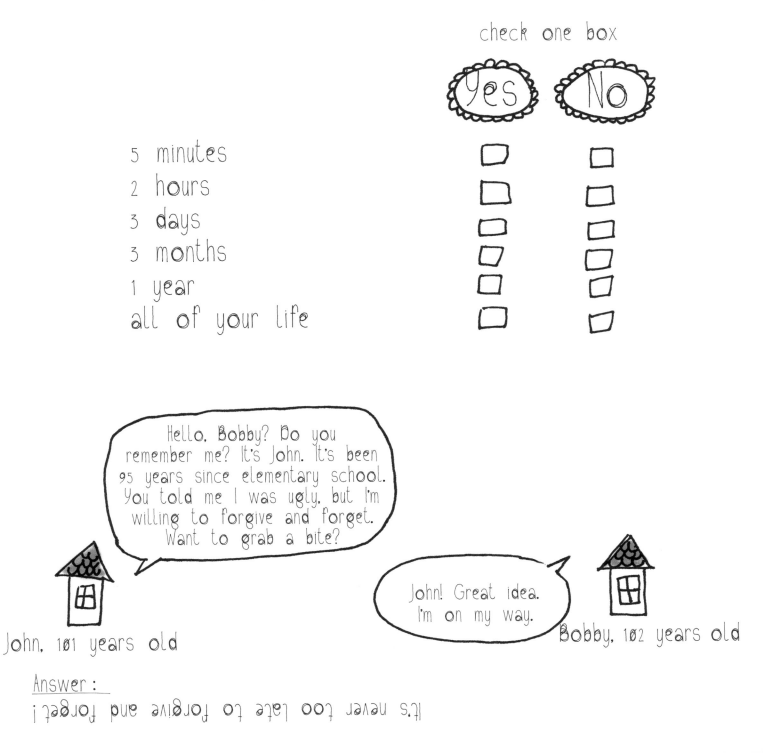

Hello, Bobby? Do you remember me? It's John. It's been 95 years since elementary school. You told me I was ugly, but I'm willing to forgive and forget. Want to grab a bite?

John! Great idea. I'm on my way.

John, 101 years old

Bobby, 102 years old

Answer:

It's never too late to forgive and forget!

Check out the
next page.
Cut out these
little phrases
and use them
the next time you
want to make up
with someone!

(This is the back of the
making up phrases page.)

# Create Amazing Business Cards!

**1** Get a piece of construction paper and cut it into 8 pieces.

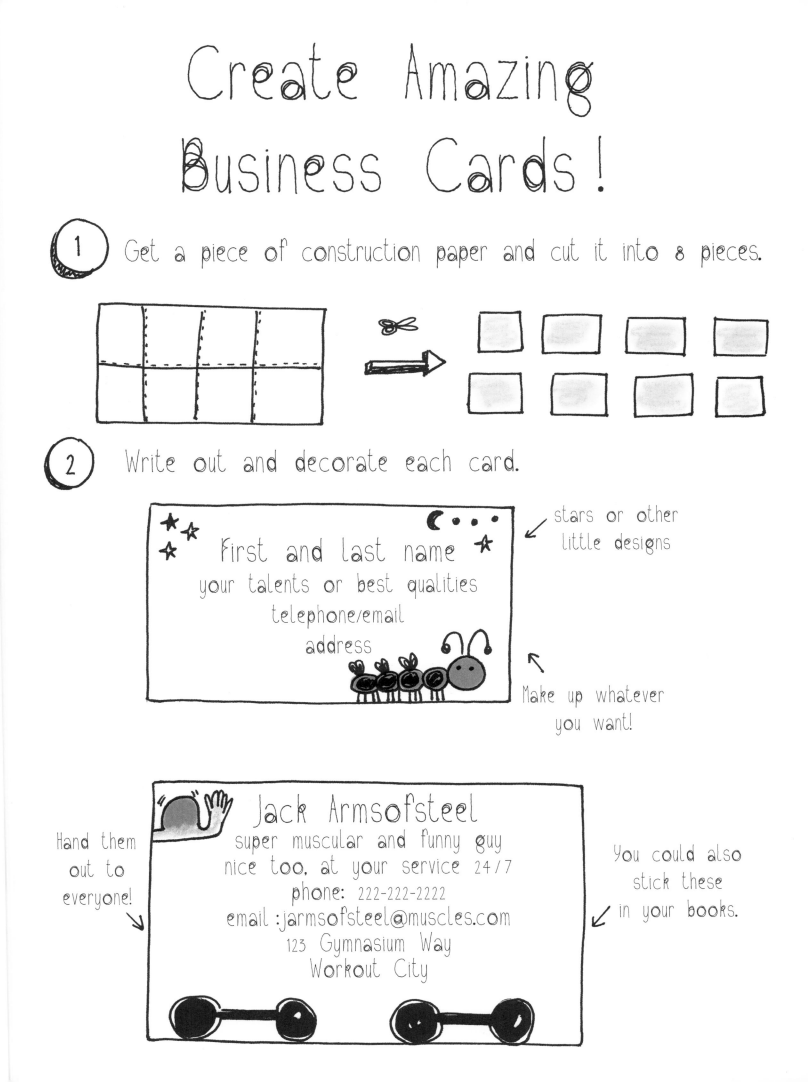

**2** Write out and decorate each card.

First and last name
your talents or best qualities
telephone/email
address

stars or other little designs

Make up whatever you want!

Jack Armsofsteel
super muscular and funny guy
nice too, at your service 24/7
phone: 222-222-2222
email :jarmsofsteel@muscles.com
123 Gymnasium Way
Workout City

Hand them out to everyone!

You could also stick these in your books.

# It's Cool to Share Stuff and Help People !

Imagine that:

**1**

You're horrible at gymnastics but you make a mean earthworm pie...

**2**

You meet a really nice gymnast who only knows how to cook rice...

You can teach her how to make your special pie, and she can teach you her gymnastics tricks!

→ Make a list of everything you know how to do really well that you could teach to other people.

examples: preparing breakfast in bed, setting up a tent, making banana milkshakes...

# For Couples Only:
## Private and Personal!

Close your eyes and think very hard about your boyfriend/girlfriend.

Do you really, really like them? . . . . . . . . .

If yes, have you liked them for a long time? . . . .

What is it about them that you like best?

. . . . . . . . . . . . . . . . . . . . . . . . .

Do they really, really like you too? . . . . . . .

Have you told anyone how you feel? . . . . . . .

Have you ever thought about kissing them? . . . . .

smack!

Answer the questions in your head if you don't want anyone to find out!

# Where would you most like to spend time with your best friend?

a  On the moon

Hotel La Luna

b  Their Parents' House

Finish your vegetables!

No talking at the table!

You need to leave by 8 p.m!

c  Camping in the wilderness

grr grr

Or, write down another idea:

# COMFORTING ADVICE

Sometimes bad things happen to good people, even if they're really good:

Your sweetheart has a crush on someone else, and you can't figure out why!

The Cheerleader →
Every girl's worst nightmare. She's waiting for the right moment to steal your boyfriend.

Class Clown
With his ability to charm people and make them laugh, you've got to watch your girlfriend around this guy.

## Or even worse!

Santa isn't going to bring you a present this year.

# QUICK TIPS FOR GETTING OVER IT

(1) Have a good cry!

(2) Write down a list of things that will take your mind off stuff and make you smile when you're feeling down.
example: a big hug

- 
- 
- 
- 

(3) Do it right away! That's an order!

# How can you stay in touch with

## Circle the <u>best answers</u>.

(a) You can invite them over for the weekend or to go on a trip.

**PRIORITY MOVERS**
When moving people counts

(b) You can pack them up and take them with you.

Check either true or false:

|  | True | False |
|---|---|---|
| Being alone allows you to daydream. | ☐ | ☐ |
| Being alone lets you explore your true feelings and state of mind. | ☐ | ☐ |
| Being alone allows your mind to wander and think about things that aren't important. | ☐ | ☐ |
| You can read books when you're alone. | ☐ | ☐ |
| You can rest when you're alone. | ☐ | ☐ |

Your huge and soggy cat that's been left out in the rain. →

Oh, I've sofa all

## people is great.
## nice to be alone!

|  | True | False |
|---|:---:|:---:|
| When you're alone, you can scratch your mosquito bites without feeling self-conscious. | ☐ | ☐ |
| Being alone lets you think about what you really want without being influenced by others. | ☐ | ☐ |
| You don't have to clean up your room if you're alone. | ☐ | ☐ |
| If you're alone you can do things you really want (like eating peanut butter out of the jar with a spoon). | ☐ | ☐ |
| When you're alone you can try out different hairstyles and admire yourself in front of the mirror. | ☐ | ☐ |

got the
to myself!

# Guess if this magic potion really works...

Bottle o' Happy

Give a spoon of this potion to someone, and in 30 seconds they will be your best friend for life!

No arguments!

No misunderstandings!

Yes ☐          No ☐

Answer:

Of course not. Friendship is hard work, and you've got to put some effort into it if you want it to thrive and grow!!!

# Hooray for Summer Camp!

Have you ever been to summer camp?

If yes, describe your fondest camp memory.

If no, would you like to go? Yes ☐ No ☐

At summer camp you can ride a pony. But have you ever tried skiing with a bear at winter camp?

This Way to Fun!

# SUPER CHALLENGE

Try spending <u>an entire day</u> without making fun of anyone, saying anything bad, or being the slightest bit sarcastic.

"Your hair is too cool! I love it! What planet is your salon on?"

<u>Before you start,</u> check a box:

pathological liar!

a ☐ Too easy. I never criticize people.

b ☐ Sounds fun. I'll give it a try. ↖ bravo!

 # THE PAGE FOR PEACE

Write down everything that goes through your mind when you think about peace.

## Now, do you REALLY think we can love everyone?

- If yes, why?

- If no, why?

# Personal Pop Quiz

If your friend needs help,
you give them:

a ☐ a shove
b ☐ a hand
c ☐ a slap
d ☐ a punch
e ☐ a pinch
f ☐ a kick in the pants

Answer:

b. Give them a hand, of course!

# How Do You Solve Problems?

Check out these drawings

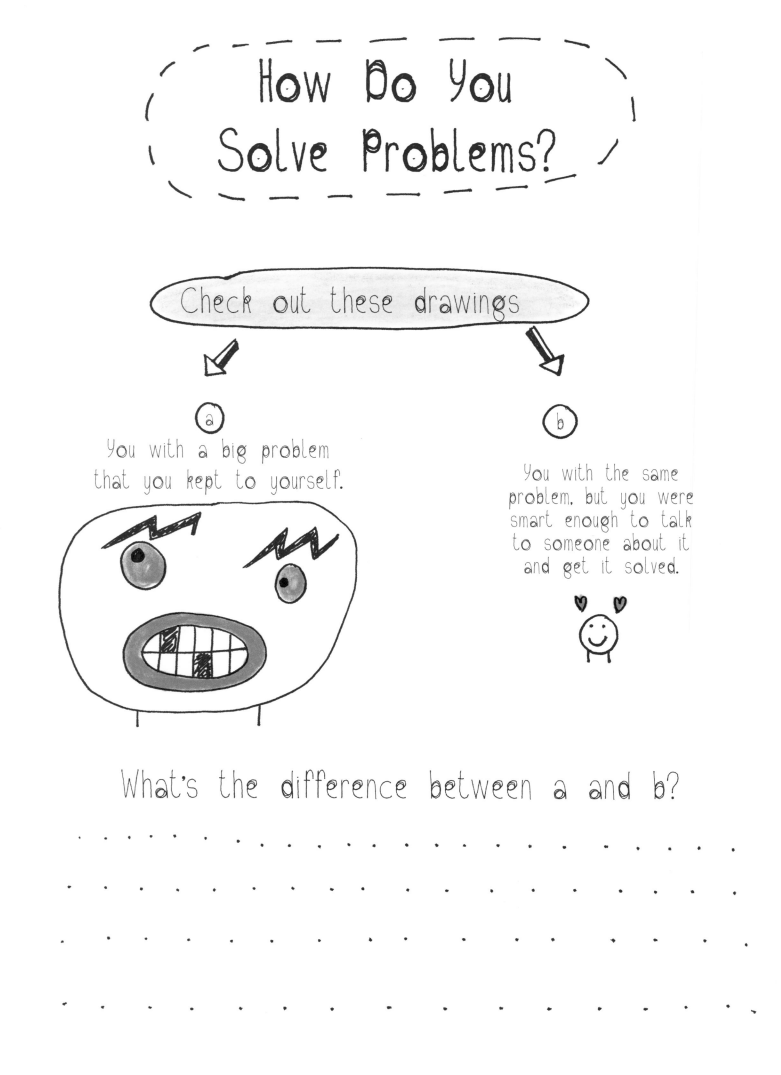

**a**

You with a big problem that you kept to yourself.

**b**

You with the same problem, but you were smart enough to talk to someone about it and get it solved.

What's the difference between a and b?

# Power Riddle!

Do you know the difference between your parents and Mr. Universe?
(He's the strongest man in the world.)

clap! clap!

washboard abs

Answer:

There is no difference. Your parents are just as strong and will support you with their powerful heart muscles!

# Stay Positive!

If your mom tells you...      and your dad says...

grrr !
Clean up your room
right now, or
I'll trade you for the
neighbors' dog !

grrr !
You're getting on my
nerves ! Go to bed
before I take away
your allowance.

## you think:

a ☐ My parents hate me! Life is so unfair.

b ☐ When are they going to calm down?
They should go look at themselves in the mirror.

c ☐ I know my parents love me. They say things they don't
mean when they're tired.

Remember

We love each other even when we are not getting along!

# IT'S THE LITTLE THINGS THAT COUNT!

Bring your parents breakfast in bed:

(The author of this book is not crazy.
She knows her kids will be reading this.)

① Pay attention to what they like to eat.

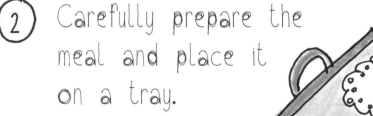
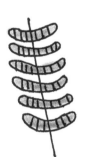

② Carefully prepare the meal and place it on a tray.

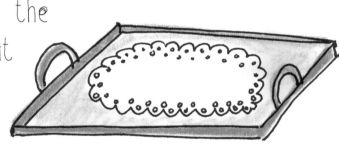

③ Don't bother with hot drinks if you've never made them before. You might burn yourself.

COUPON
Good for one cup of coffee.

# TICK TOCK! TIME FOR BREAKFAST!

Draw pictures of your parents completely full and lying in bed. Add their comments in the bubbles.

Now's the time if you want to ask them something. Quick! Do it before it's too late.

# The Family That Plays Together, Stays Together.

 **1** The rules: Everyone makes an effort to smile, be gracious and friendly.

(example: No biting, no fighting and absolutely no bullying your brothers or sisters.)

**2** All participants (parents and children) promise to respect the rules and sign here:

| Name | Signature |
|------|-----------|
|      |           |

**3** Make funny posters and tape them all over the house. (Don't forget the bathroom door.)

example:

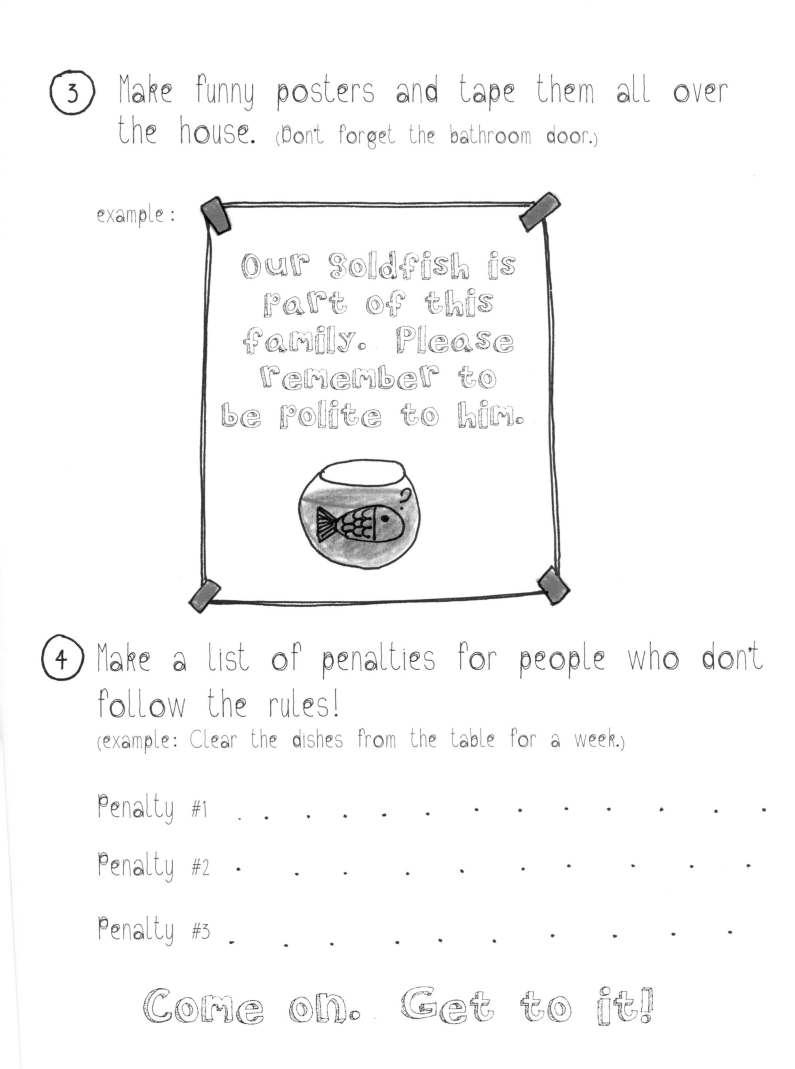

Our goldfish is part of this family. Please remember to be polite to him.

**4** Make a list of penalties for people who don't follow the rules!
(example: Clear the dishes from the table for a week.)

Penalty #1 . . . . . . . . . . . . . . . .

Penalty #2 . . . . . . . . . . . . . . . .

Penalty #3 . . . . . . . . . . . . . . . .

Come on. Get to it!

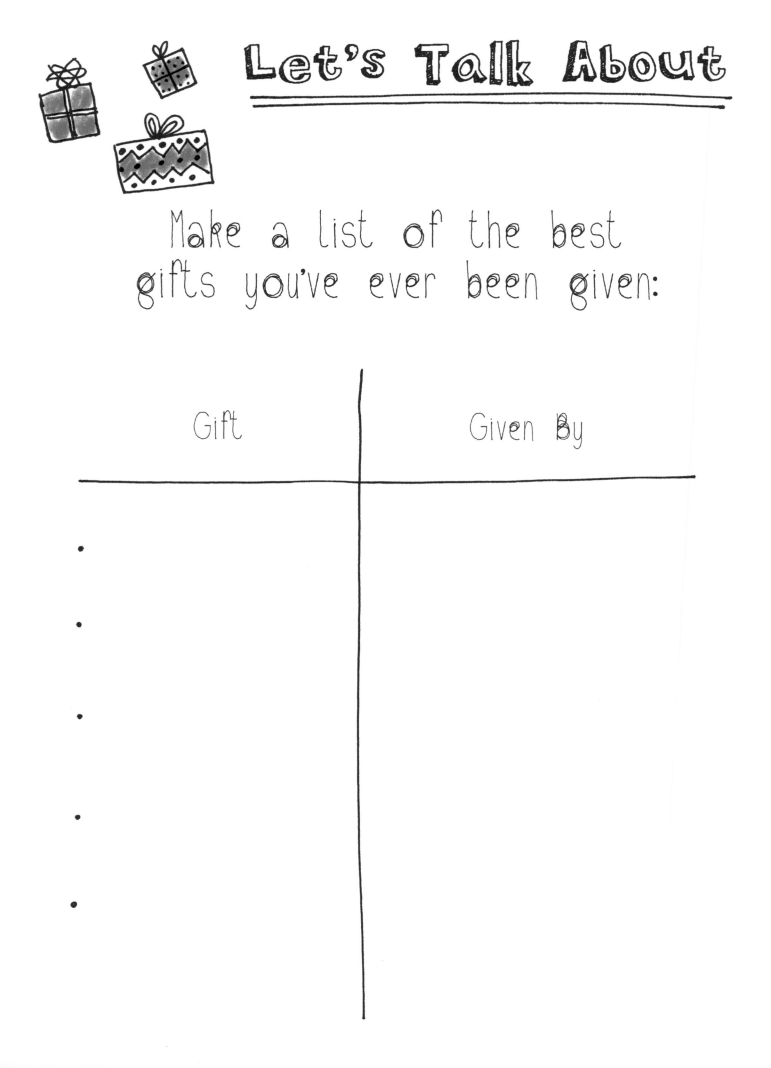

# Let's Talk About

Make a list of the best gifts you've ever been given:

| Gift | Given By |
|------|----------|
| • | |
| • | |
| • | |
| • | |
| • | |

# Generosity...

## And a list of those that you gave:

| Gift | Given to |
|------|----------|
| example: Necklace of macaroni | Mom |

- 
- 
- 
- 
-

# What about

CIRCLE THE GIFTS
THAT COST NOTHING!

* a smile
* a helping hand
* an invitation
* a big hug
* imaginary shoes
* the air that you breathe
* a compliment
* a camera
* good advice
* a soft green lawn to do cartwheels on

# priceless gifts?

Hey, kitty. You know what? The best gifts usually don't cost a thing, and they don't come from a store.

Yes, you're right! Like mice, for example! . . .

# How to Make a Treasure Box

1) Trace the example below. 2) Cut around the outside edges.
3) Cut along the 6 blue lines. 4) Fold along the black lines.
5) Put glue on the 4 areas that are shaded blue. 6) Place a surprise inside and secure the box with a ribbon, colorful tape or stickers.

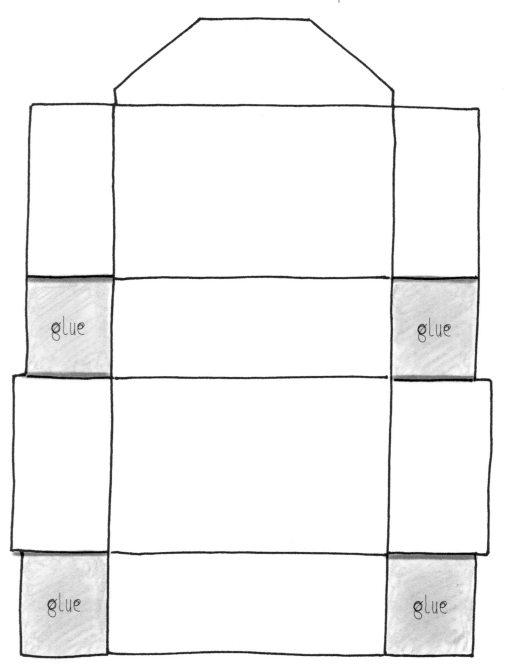

Inside, you could put...

Your dad's favorite chocolates

A coupon for something

Coupon for 1 kiss

Hamster poop, for your worst enemy!

A ring for your mom or best friend

**yuck! gross!
(just kidding!)**

# Test : Are You Very

Old lady Johnson,
125 years old

## example #1

A little old lady climbs aboard the bus
with a huge grocery cart.

a ☐ You get up and offer her your seat.
b ☐ You tell her she can sit on your lap.
c ☐ You pretend that you don't see her.

## example #2

When you enter a store:

a ☐ You see that someone is coming in after you,
and you smile and hold the door open.
b ☐ You barely hold the door with your fingertips
and scream, "Come on. I'm in a hurry!!!"
c ☐ You pay no attention and let the door slam into
the person coming in behind you.

# Considerate?

Good evening!

We're here!

Mr. and Mrs. Deadhead

### example #3

Your parents invite their best friends, Mr. and Mrs. Deadhead, over for dinner.

a ☐ You hide under your bed.

b ☐ You welcome them by screaming, "Hey, great to see you!!"

c ☐ You pay your respects, but end up putting a whoopee cushion on Mr. Deadhead's chair and your pet rat in Mrs. Deadhead's purse.

Answers:

example #3: Whatever you want. They really are a weird couple.

example #1: a  example #2 a

# What Would You Do with Superpowers?

a ☐ Fly to Hollywood to have dinner with your favorite movie star.

b ☐ Help all the needy people in the world.

c ☐ Create a clone, kick back in bed and send the clone to school.

HOLLYWOOD

Limo with pool.
↓

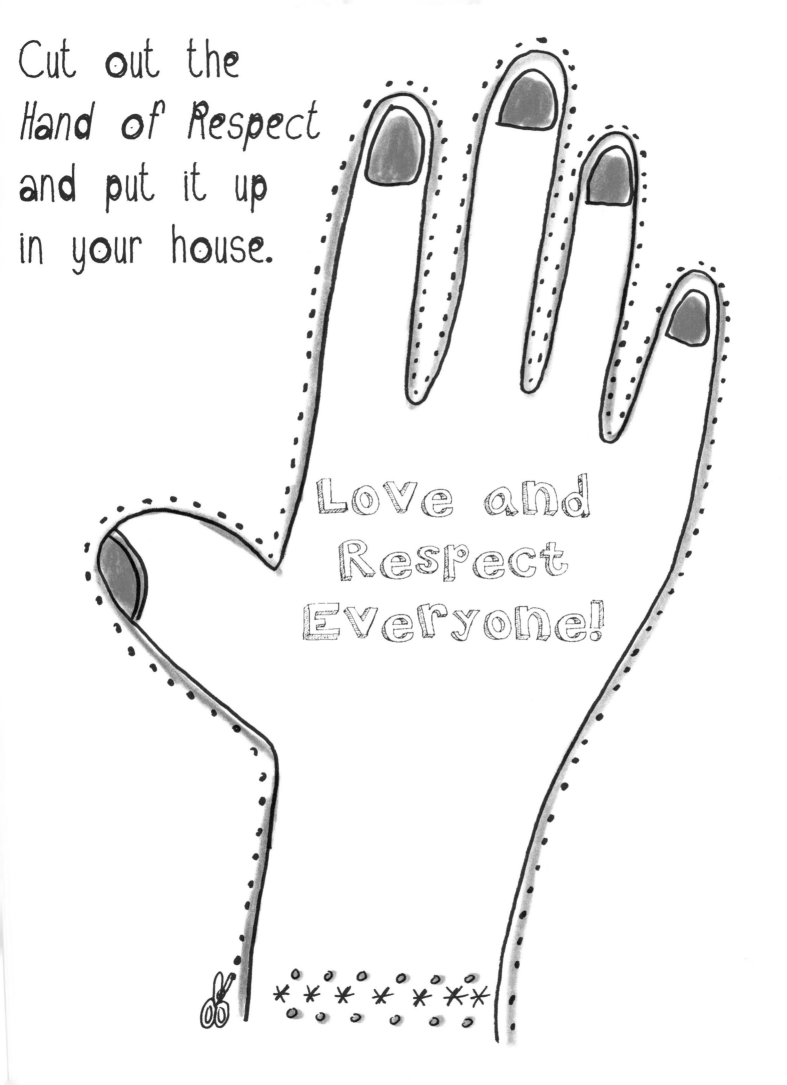

(This is the back
of the *Hand of Respect*.)

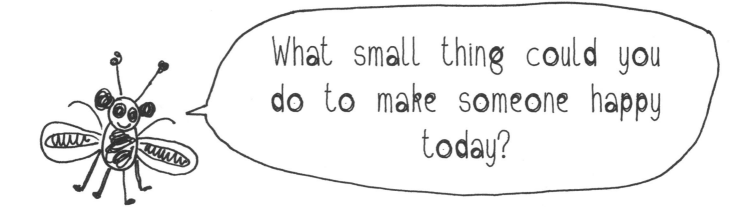

# So? What did you think of this book?

Cool ☐

Amazing ☐

Loved it ☐

Whatever ☐

↑

Watch it! If you check this box you're going to change into a crazy little alien.

For Lou, Gabin, Clémentine, Chloé and Marco ♥

First American Edition 2011
Kane Miller, A Division of EDC Publishing

First published in France under the title J'aime les autres by hélium, 12, rue de l'Arbalète 75005 Paris
Copyright © 2010, hélium editions

All rights reserved.
For information contact:
Kane Miller, A Division of EDC Publishing
P.O. Box 470663
Tulsa, OK 74147-0663
www.kanemiller.com
www.edcpub.com

Library of Congress Control Number: 2010941479

Manufactured by Regent Publishing Services, Hong Kong
Printed April 2011 in ShenZhen, Guangdong, China
1 2 3 4 5 6 7 8 9 10
ISBN: 978-1-61067-012-8